Surfer's Start-Up:

A Beginner's Guide to Surfing

Second Edition

Masterson

By
Doug Werner

Start-Up Sports #1

Tracks Publishing
San Diego, California

Cover photo credit (clockwise from upper right): Weber, McClain, Werner, Werner

Surfer's Start-Up:
A Beginner's Guide to Surfing
Second Edition
By Doug Werner

Start-Up Sports / Tracks Publishing
140 Brightwood Avenue
Chula Vista, CA 91910
619-476-7125 Fax 619-476-8173
http://www.startupsports.com

Publisher's Cataloging in Publication

Werner, Doug, 1950-
    Surfer's start-up : a beginner's guide to
surfing / by Doug Werner. – 2nd ed.
    p. cm. – (Start-up sports ; #1)
    Includes bibliographical references and index.
    LCCN: 99-70979.
    ISBN: 1-884654-12-6

    1. Surfing.   I. Title.   II. Series.

GV840.S8W47 1999   797.3'2
                    QBI99-383

To Kathleen

Werner

Acknowledgements

Stu Kenson
Robin Niehaus
David Montalbano
Jim Montalbano
Diane Gallo
Craig McClain
Christine Gillard
Mike Gillard
Gene Wheeler
Genie Wheeler
LeRoy Grannis
Vance Masterson
Todd Westfall
South Juanita Surf Club
Jeff Phillips
Kathy Phillips
Craig Colburn
Steve Hawk
Dori Payne
Mary Lou Drummy
Cliff Schlabach
Roxanne Schlabach
Black Sheep
Dan Poynter
Court Overin
Jay Novak
Pat Weber
Lynne Weber
ColorType
Jim Clinkscales
Phyllis Carter
Red Werner
Ann Werner
Tim Sutherland
Bob Sutherland

Preface

I began writing this book because I knew it would be fun. As I got rolling, I realized I had something to say. Perhaps there is a real need for this guide. Most of us learn on our own. I didn't see any "How-to-Surf" books around.

Since somebody was bound to read it, I also figured I could attempt to instill some attitude in this thing. Mostly respect. For surfers already in the water, for the situation that exists, for the sport I love so much. This book is easy to read, big on pictures and light in spirit. It's put together in broad strokes designed to get you out in the water and give it a go. It's loose in its treatment of anything historical, oceanographic or technical. But you'll get the picture.

I hope my surfing buddies don't turn on me or ridicule my efforts too much. But I expect it. From now on, every time I fall off someone is going to hand me this book. Anyway, have fun with it. If you take it up, be good to the sport, to the surfers who came before and to yourself.

Doug Werner

Sutherland

As in other sports, determination and desire can help power your trip through the learning curve. Think about Tim Sutherland when you're trying to ride your first waves. He surfs everyday in Imperial Beach, California with an artificial foot.

Contents

Preface   5
Introduction: The Meat of the Matter   9

1. Gear   15
2. The Right Waves   23
3. Safety   29
4. Rules of the Road   35
5. Pre-Paddle   41
6. Paddling   47
7. Catching a Wave   55
8. Angling   65
9. Waves   71
10. Crowds, Localism & You   79
11. What Now?   85
12. A Little History   91
13. Interview:
    Pat Weber: San Diego's Surfing Coach   103

Glossary   109
Resources   113
Bibliography   122
Index   123

Sexy stuff.

The Meat of the Matter

This is a book for **beginners** — People who would like to learn how to surf but have little or no experience with surfing or even the ocean. When I was collecting testimonials for the first edition back in 1993, I was told by a former world champion and the current head honcho of one of the major surfing tours that it was a "beginnah's beginning book" (he's Australian). He got it right.

It's a straightforward guide without the insider surfer's slang. As the *Library Journal* said, "Werner generally eschews the cutesy surfin' safari lingo that often plagues books such as this." They got it right. We are trying to *reach* people here. Not to impress or confuse. (Eschew, by the way, means to shun or avoid. I had to look it up since it was such a gnarly term.)

Surfer's Start-Up is a simple, almost Dick and Jane approach to surfing instruction that works. Our book is not very sexy, although, as one esteemed reviewer put it, we "get to the meat of the matter." That is, we will teach you how to stand up on a surfboard. And *that* is very exciting (even sexy!) indeed.

Special care was taken to photograph our surfers in small beach break surf, suitable for learning. This kind of surf can be found on any coast around the world given the right tide, wind and swell conditions. We could have illustrated the book with David Montalbano and Christine Gillard (the models in this book) riding perfect, eight-foot waves like in the magazines, but everyday beginners aren't likely to encounter such surf, let alone negotiate it.

Global

A zillion people surf today. All over the world. Wherever there's a coastline — the USA (even *Alaska* ... even the *Great Lakes*), Canada, Mexico, Central America, South America, Japan, Vietnam, Australia, New Zealand, Africa, Europe ... Did I say you needed a coastline? I'm sorry. They're building wave pools in Arizona, Nevada, and in all sorts of hot, high and/or dry places. This is especially wondrous to those of us who first came to surfing when it was really a Hawaiian and Southern Californian thing.

The modern age of surfing is around 50 years old. Maybe 60. LeRoy Grannis, famed surfing photographer and ageless wonder remembers *not* paddling out at Malibu once because his friends couldn't make it. He showed me a photo of the surf that day. It was six feet and flawless. No surfers at Malibu is like no one showing up for the Super Bowl. It doesn't happen. It's hard to imagine that not so long ago surfing was a *secret*.

Lifers

Since surfing has been with us for a few years, surfers are of all ages ... from 6 to 70. Like rock music, it isn't an adolescent pastime anymore. I'm 48. Twenty years

Grannis Collection

Legendary surfing photog LeRoy Grannis surfs every day at 80-something. *That's* inspiration.

ago, that was pretty old in any lineup. However, I've paddled out at some places in recent years and felt out of place because I didn't look like Santa Claus. Just like endeavors in any walk of life, age means less and less as folks take better care of themselves and listen to their hearts. Who says you can't surf at seventy?

Respectable

Surfers are also, ahh...what's the word ... respectable. Off the top of my head, I know of two city mayors, one Shakespearean actor, three millionaires, six published authors, one legendary tycoon and a Hollywood director — all who surf. I've met lawyers, doctors, dentists, nurses, teachers, artists, NFL players, major league baseball players and a couple United States Representatives — all who surf.

It's not exactly like meeting someone who golfs, but then it's not like striking up a conversation with a mad bomber, either. And believe me, surfers were held in the worst light for many years (not that they didn't enjoy the notoriety or encourage the wrath of mid-century, white-bread America — we did!)

To think that surfers were once equated with juvenile delinquency or the counter culture is truly laughable. But then today's popular image of a surfer is Bart Simpson-esque (Hey Dude!). Go figure.

The point is (I think): Everybody surfs or has surfed or will surf or *wants* to surf. Everybody, everywhere. And I can prove it.

But that's another book.

Sex

You don't have to be a male to surf. Half the photos in this book show former National Champion Christine Gillard* demonstrating technique. She is not alone. Although the waves are disproportionately crowded

McClain

Move over fellas.

with guys, women are making a stronger and stronger showing in the water. (Go for it ladies. Christine is better than 95% of the guys in the water and she doesn't even surf every day.)

Yikes!

This book is about how to surf both physically and morally (yikes!) It's simple, short and straight to the point. Since there are so many of us now, maybe this book is timely and will strike a nail on the head.

Let's hit it!

*Christine was National Scholastic Surfing Association (NSSA) National Champion in 1985, 1986 and 1991. She was also U.S. Amateur Champion in 1986.

David Montalbano, our other featured surfer, has equally impressive credentials having placed high in numerous professional and amateur contests. He is currently working in Los Angeles as an actor and screen writer.

McClain

Dave is holding up two surfboards, topside to camera. This is the side surfers stand on and need to wax in order not to slip. The larger board on the right is the beginner's best bet. Notice its length and width. For a novice Dave's size, the small board won't float or paddle adequately. The cord at the base of the board is the leash.

Gear

The Right Surfboard

The right surfboard to learn on is big enough for you to paddle easily and to sit on comfortably without sinking. ***This is crucial!*** Get a board at least as tall as your hand raised above your head, about three inches thick and 22 inches wide in the middle. Think big, fat and ugly. Avoid the small, thin models (which are prevalent) because you'll spend all your time fighting them. A board taller than your reach is fine. Just remember a much bigger board is more difficult to transport and manage in the surf. Make sure it fits under your arm and that you can carry it.

Sponge is Good!

In the first edition I said this about soft, beginner boards:

Avoid those spongy, beginner boards. Although softer and safer, the feel of a sponge boat is just too weird. Get a real surfboard made of foam and fiberglass. You'll be safe enough if you use your head.

Modern soft beginner boards provide safety and flotation to first time riders. They don't look like the potato chips that pros ride, but hey, you'll get up on your feet!

Now I say:

There are soft novice boards available that surfing instructors and their students swear by. These sponge boards hurt less when they hit and have rounded fins that will not cut. Because they don't bash or slice, the beginner may venture into his or her lesson with more confidence. They're designed to surf pretty good for newcomers and the more modern shapes are recommended. Early sponge board models really sucked.

However, it's still true that all beginners graduate to foam and fiberglass, just like you went from a bike with training wheels to without. Soft boards are training devices and it's not necessary that you learn on one. You can learn successfully on a real foam and fiberglass surfboard *if it's the right size and shape for you.*

Here are the same two boards, held sideways. Note the thicknesses. Your board should be fat, like the one on the right. Fins are located on the tail of the surfboard and enable surfers to turn. No, they aren't handles.

And these are the bottoms of the surfboards. We don't wax here. The small board has three fins for greater turning capabilities. This is very common. The single fin is a somewhat outdated concept. Fin arrangements mean nothing to the beginner. Just make sure you have at least one.

McClain

McClain

Make sure your board floats well. Christine's surfboard is so small it sinks when she sits on it. It's OK for someone at her level of expertise, but for the beginner it will be difficult to surf on or even to sit on comfortably.

Finding This Board

Find a surf shop in your area that rents. For a few bucks you can try a board before buying one and get a feel for the size and shape you'll ultimately need. Check out the selection. Notice how beat up they look. This is their last stop before the dumpster. Bow your head in silence and appreciation for the lives they've led and find one that's big, fat and ugly enough for you. Don't be swayed by looks.

If you can't find anything on the racks that's the right size and shape, try another shop. It will do no good to settle for anything less. Try asking around. The surfers at the shop or perhaps the surfers at the beach may know of something. You should be able to locate one that's right for you. Surfboards are plentiful and finding one that will work at this stage in your budding surfing career should be easy.

Wetsuit

Everybody wears wetsuits most of the time these days. They're colorful, fashionable and cover wayward flesh. Unless you've swallowed a beach ball, they make most of us look like wave argonauts.

They also keep you toasty. With them you can stay in the water longer. Wetsuits work by allowing some water in the suit. That's why they're called "wet" suits. Once inside a snug suit, water is warmed by your body and acts as a hot water bottle.

In case you're wondering, wearing one is not a problem. There was a time when wearing rubber was cumbersome, but today's wetsuits are miracles of modern science — they're light, flexible and comfortable.

Obviously, if the air temperature is 75, the water temperature 75 and the wind calm, you won't need or want a wetsuit. You may want to wear a T-shirt or a nylon slipover if your skin is sensitive to the waxed surface of your board.

If a suit is desirable, look to rent. If you cannot rent one, buy a used one. Again, don't go for looks. Just make sure there aren't holes in it and that it fits snugly. Not so tight you turn red, but that it j-u-s-t stretches across limbs and torso. Baggy suits won't work.

Wax

Wax is rubbed on the deck or topside of the board to prevent slipping. Your board may have traction patches slapped on the deck. Don't wax those. Buy surf wax at the surf shop or at convenience stores near the beach. There are numerous brands. For now, anything will do.

Leash

Get a leash. It's an elastic cord that attaches to your ankle and connects you to the surfboard. It keeps the board around when you wipe out (fall off) and prevents "killer board." This is a leash-less board thundering toward a hapless surfer or swimmer in a wall of white water. The adjective "killer" here isn't to be confused with the adjective "killer" in, say, "killer chick" or "killer flick." Rental boards will probably come with one. Buy an inexpensive one if you have to.

Racks (Maybe)

If you have to drive with your surfboard, and it won't fit in your car without sticking too far out, you'll need racks. Hopefully you can rent some, but if not, buy a cheap set that can go on and off easily. Don't leave them on the car when you go surfing.

The Generous Hawaiian

Believe me, I know surf shops can be intimidating. When I was 12 everyone in the shop was older, had cool hair and wore the perfect T-shirt. I couldn't understand much of anything they said and, in general, felt like a real suburbanite in the land of adolescent nirvana.

When I was 22, I had the look and the hair. Even the

talk. But no money.

Now I've got the money and a lot less hair. Yet, once again, I can't understand what the guys behind the counter are saying. And worse — I know they're better surfers than I am.

But no matter. You see, at my advanced age, I've discovered that even those who work in surf shops are people. And capable of remarkable things. Case in point. I was in Maui, December of 1987, without my board. Don't ask why. Somehow I thought I'd do other things or something. Until I saw the surf.

I remember looking at these huge peaks and feeling the hairs at the nape of my neck stand up like my dog's when he sees a cat or a vacuum cleaner. It was time to visit the local shop.

I headed straight for the rental racks but there was nothing there except an old ironing board. So I decided to buy. Now you've got to understand that I'm cheap by nature, and for me to spend anything over $25 is serious stuff. However, "there are times" and this definitely was one.

By and by, the fellow watching the store came around to help. He was a local boy and probably ate 30-foot waves and California white boys like me for breakfast. But I didn't care. I had my gold card and was deep in a modest frenzy.

He listened to my babble with a smile and said (this is absolutely true), "You look like a nice guy and know what's what. Take this board here for five dollars a day. Try not to ding it and bring it back in a week." The surfboard was a perfect 6'8" Linden, immaculate, with a price tag of $375. This is the kind of surfboard that people openly admire when you paddle out. And this guy, this local who was supposed to hate me for infesting his surfing area, is renting it to me for *five dollars a day*. All I could figure was the fellow saw my burning desire and responded like a very friendly fellow surfer. And an extraordinarily generous one.

You probably shouldn't expect such miracles from your local shop. But understand that underneath the thin shells of arrogance lurk real folks who may help you if you show off your desire and courtly manners.

The RIGHT Waves

Whatcha Gotta Have
There are two things you'll **absolutely** need in order to learn how to surf. One, the **right surfboard**. Two, the **right waves**. Chapter One described what you need to surf on — a big, fat, ugly surfboard. In this section, I'll describe what conditions you need to surf in.

Finding a Spot
Let's make it as easy as possible. Visit the surf spots in your area. Go where the surfers go and take a good look. Avoid spots that are difficult to get to. You don't need to deal with cliffs, rocks or long hikes to the beach. Look for a sandy beach next to a parking lot.

Check out the size of the surf. Try to learn on small days — hip high or less. All you really need at this stage is something that breaks and has a little push. Look at the waves. What you want are waves that spill or crumble down their faces. Not waves that break top to bottom, all at once. Obviously, the waves should break some distance from shore at a decent depth.

These are **ideal conditions** in which to learn: The waves are small and easy breaking. There are very few surfers out.

Now look at the surfers in the water. Find the best ones and note where they sit. **You will <u>not</u> paddle out there.** Look up or down the beach from the experts and try to find a less crowded spot, hopefully with beginners like you. Watch them. Is the paddle out easy? When they try to stand, do they make it or does the wave demolish them? Remember that easy does it for now. Easy paddle out into easy, gentle surf. If the waves are too big and powerful — **wait!** The swell will die down eventually. Try again another day. It's no bueno to paddle out in strong surf the first day. You'll only get discouraged and battered.

First Encounters
Talk to surfers in the surf shops and on the beach. Don't be afraid to ask where the best novice break is.

This is a **spilling wave** — a good wave to learn on. The wave is breaking easily down the face. Sort of crumbly-like.

This is a **top-to-bottom wave** — a bad wave to learn on. The wave is breaking hard because it's pitching its peak and plunging top to bottom — all at once. Note its cylindrical or tube-like form — always a telltale sign of a top-to-bottom wave.

Note: These photos were taken at the same location — the spilling wave at high tide and the top-to-bottom wave at low tide. This is the difference a tide can make.

They'll be happy you're not going to thrash about near them. This, by the way, may be your first contact with surfers whom you'll eventually share the better waves after you're a bit more experienced. So put on a good face! Exude desire, enthusiasm and courtesy. You're paying your dues starting now. Show respect and

25

humility. As you improve, your chances of breaking into the lineup will be greater if they remember you as the beginner who once asked humbly where you could best learn. You may be a kook (beginner), but you are one who shows respect.

Anything for the Ladies

Learning to surf in small waves is also a good idea for the instructor. Twice I've taught people in surf conditions a tad too powerful for a comfortable learning experience. Paddling out was just too much for the students who had all they could handle just pointing the board in the right direction.

Being the he-man that I think I am, I towed the students outside the breaking waves. It should be noted that the instructees were nubile young ladies and the same service would not be accorded to the guys. Sex discrimination? You bet.

When I say tow, that's not with a rope and a boat. But a rope and a dope: me. By the time I had dragged the ladies out twice, I was ready for the paramedics. It's all a little hazy, but I do believe they both stood up and went away totally jazzed.

$$\longrightarrow$$

Life of a Wave.
This sequence of shots shows a wave as a line of swell, peaking, breaking and peeling down its length. This is a spilling wave with good form. These are terrific conditions in which to learn.

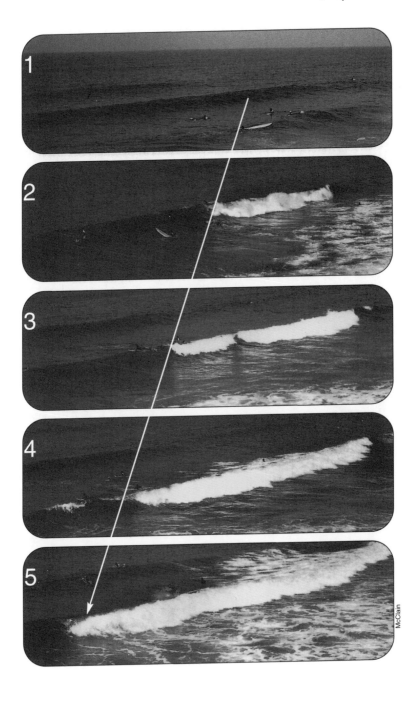

McClain

Masterson

<u>Not</u> a good day to paddle.

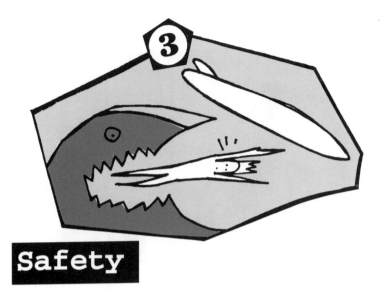

Safety

Learn How to Swim

Most waves break in large bodies of water. You should feel confident and comfortable in your ability to go from point A to point B in the surf and open ocean.

Watch Out!

You're just learning. Keep things safe and simple. Surfboards can bash and slice. Stay away from other surfers in the beginning. If you can't avoid them entirely, put as much distance as possible between yourself and others. Don't paddle behind anybody. Don't take off (catch a wave) with anybody. Don't take off on top of anybody. **Be aware** of where you are, where they are and where the waves are —
all the time!

Board Control

Wear a leash. Your board should have one, but if it doesn't, get one. Besides keeping your board if you wipe out, a leash prevents it from making a death swoop into the beach. This does not mean you can let

A leash-less board can be a **killer board** if lost.

the board go at will. **Hold onto your board!** The leash allows destruction in a ten-foot radius and may snap back with ugly results.

When you wipe out, always feel for the tug on your leash or lack thereof. If it tugs, cover yourself in that direction and wait for the strain to subside. That means the board won't snap back. But also be aware of the tug-less leash. Your board may be just above you on the surface. Resurface with hands over your head to prevent a collision.

Wiping Out
When you wipe out, the board will usually go its own way and you another. The leash will hold on to your wayward surfboard, tug at your ankle and nestle a few feet away. You'll plop yourself back onto the board and resume your graceless performance. However, until you really get into the know, whenever you fall off, cover your head. Don't drop your hands until you've resurfaced and see your surfboard. Don't dive straight down,

Wiping Out —Dave's board has pearled, or nose-dived, because he had too much weight forward. He covers his head in order to protect himself from his board. This is a wipe-out. You'll get good at this.

Dave has resurfaced from the same wipe-out with his head still protected. These precautions are a bit exaggerated, but it's a good idea to be cautious until you get a good feel for things.

especially headfirst. The water may be shallow. Sand bar diving is unintelligent and quite painful. Sort of lean into your wipe out. You'll get good at wiping out a lot faster than riding.

Caught Inside
If you're caught inside (inside the breaking waves) and someone's board is going to hit you ... **dive**. The board may be bashed, but better it than you. Again, as you resurface keep your hands over your head. Remember, this time you have two boards *and* a thrashing body to contend with.

Lobster Traps
Watch out for lobster traps and their lines. Every year, surfers get their leashes caught in them and drown.

Surfing Alone
Not that it will happen a lot, but it's one of the best things in the world to do by yourself. However, it's not a particularly safe practice, since no one will be around to help you uncork your head from the reef. Don't surf alone for now.

Sunblock
It doesn't prevent cancer put it does prevent burn. Monitor your time in the sun.

Currents, Riptides
Big surf brings in this kind of moving water. If it's small, it shouldn't be a concern. Strong swells may sweep you up or down the beach, depending on their direction. This isn't dangerous unless you fall asleep and crash into a jetty or pier piling. Usually it just makes for a lot of paddling.

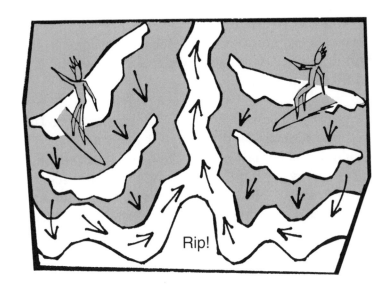

When lots of water is thrust upon the shore by breaking waves, it often finds its way back by forming rivers headed out to sea. These are rips. If you get caught in one, paddle parallel to the beach until you pop out. Don't paddle straight in against it.

Be Smart

Remember safety is more a common sense thing than a collection of valuable tips. Since you're beginning you'll want to avoid:

Big surf — Ideal surf for you is hip high or smaller, with all the force of a large puppy's swipe.

Rocky shorelines, reefs, or anything jagged or hard in or under the water — Nice sandy beaches, please.

Crowded lineups — Stay off to the side.

Oh God I'm gonna die!

It makes sense not to paddle against a rip alone at
night in the fog. Here's a story about a fellow who did
and lived to tell about it.

It was just past sunset one foggy winter's evening. The
swell was running about three to five feet and I
thought I was the last one out. As usual, I was waiting
for one last wave, but it was getting difficult to see.
Then I heard ... "Oh God! I'm gonna die!" I couldn't see
him at first, so I paddled in the direction of the voice.
Through the advancing fog, I saw a surfer paddling
hard in the direction of shore but going ... out to sea.

This was a classic case of someone getting caught in a
rip and attempting to paddle against it. Because he was
trying so hard, yet finding himself being swept to sea,
panic had set in. Panic means being frightened, of
course, but more importantly it means mindlessness.
People forget to think just when they really should.
Anyway, I got his attention and told him to paddle
toward me. That is, sideways or parallel to shore. The
rip was no more than 20 feet wide. He popped right
out!

I told him to catch the next wave and just ride in on
his belly. He lost his board (what, no leash?) on the first
wave he tried to ride, so I gave him mine. He finally
shot in, I swam in and all was well. Yes, he was very
lucky.

Rules of the Road

At least remember these two things:
1) **Treat others as you would have them treat you.**
2) **BE AWARE.**

Paddle <u>behind</u> the rider

Paddling Out
Make sure you paddle out to either side of the lineup (where surfers sit, waiting for waves). **Do not paddle straight out into the crowd.** When surfers take off, they want to see peaking walls, not some kook in the impact zone (where waves break). If you have no choice, or get caught inside, be aware of surfers taking off. Notice his or her direction and **get out of the**

35

way. If you must, paddle behind the surfer and take the brunt of the broken wave. It's dead wrong to paddle over the swell in front of a surfer's path just to avoid the soup. This is a courtesy that will be well remembered.

In the Lineup

The lineup is often a moving thing. Especially at beach breaks. Waves don't approach the shore at exactly the same place every time. At reefs or point breaks, the lineup shifts according to the size of the waves, although take-off points are considerably more predictable than at beach breaks. At any rate, once you're in the lineup, a certain amount of moving around is going to happen. At beach breaks, you'll paddle hundreds of yards along the shore on some days.

Some moving around doesn't cut it, however. Say you've been waiting for a left (wave that breaks to the left as you face the beach). You've seen it come in at this spot for a few sets, you're in position ... and here it comes! As you begin to paddle into the wave, the guy next to you (but initially farther out of position) furiously paddles around you to get at the peak. This sort of maneuvering is not cool. This is hardly much better than the ultimate rip ...

Cutting Someone Off

... or snaking is when one surfer drops in front of another surfer who has already caught the wave. Riding twosies was cute in 1958, but not anymore. This is a concrete rule: **The surfer closest to the peak should have the wave.** Unless he's too far back. Dropping in on someone who's too far back is a

McClain

Christine is **cutting off or snaking** Dave. He intends to turn to his right but she's taking off in front of him. More pix next page.

Dave clearly has the right-of-way because he's closer to the peak and stood sooner. Christine has executed the cardinal sin in surfing.

judgment call. But if you see him or her get axed or fall off, go for it. If you do take off, and he or she makes it, pull out.

Taking Off
You're taking off on a wave and you see a surfer struggling in the impact zone. They can't or won't get out of the way. Don't take off.

Watch Where You're Going!
Always be aware of the surfers around you — side to side, front and back. Nothing is more irritating than some frenzied chipmunk who spins around and takes off without looking. As you paddle around in the lineup and catch waves, watch out!

Hold On to Your Board
You're going to get caught inside. It's a part of surfing. Waves are going to break in front of you and on you. You have a responsibility to maintain control of your board. Surfers will be paddling around you. A loose board can hurt big time. Fins slice like a knife.

Just because you have a leash doesn't give you license to let the board go. Sure, it's tied to your ankle, but the cord does stretch and eliminates any and all competition within ten feet. So hold on to your board. As the white water approaches, head straight into the wave and get a grip.

Learn to **snap** from belly to feet in an athletic crouch. This is a **critical** skill. Without it you'll forever be out of sync with the waves you try to catch.

Werner

Pre-Paddle

Pop-ups

The act of standing up on your board is quick as a blink. Look at some surfers. They paddle into a wave and ... pop up! That's what you're going to do and practice before you paddle out.

Lie face down on the floor or beach. Push yourself up with your hands and swing your feet underneath you. Stand quickly into a crouch with one foot in front and knees slightly bent. There aren't any stages to this movement. Feet should be a bit wider than shoulder width. Your back foot should be at right angles to what will be the length of the board. Your front foot should point a little forward. Practice until you master a quick and smooth motion into the proper standing position.

After you've done a few of these, you'll discover what you are. Not in a metaphysical way, but if you are a regular or goofy foot. Left foot forward is regular foot, right foot forward is goofy foot. It's a natural preference, like being right- or left-handed, so disregard the names as having any meaning.

McClain

Pop-ups — Practice popping up to your feet at home and on the beach. Going from belly to an athletic stance is one quick and smooth motion. On the opposite page Christine demonstrates a pop-up on a wave.

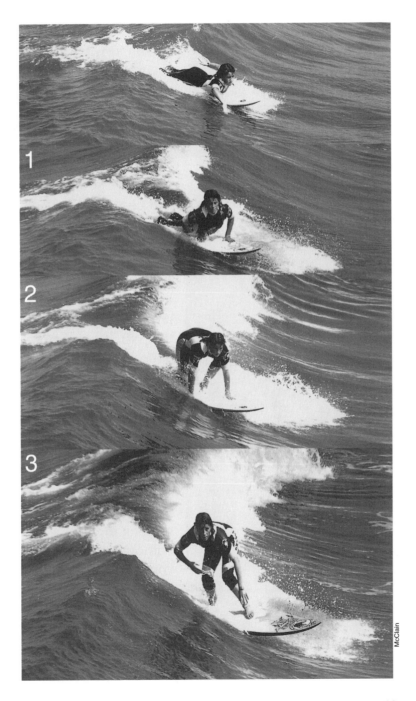

McClain

Waxing
Your rental will probably have gobs of old wax caked
on it. That's OK as long as you can comfortably lie on
the board. If the wax has become slick or there are
bare spots where you're going to lie or stand, rub on
some wax. Rub until you begin to see it form into
beads. Don't worry about the front quarter of the
board.

Wax melts. Keep the board out of the sun and the deck
down when not in use.

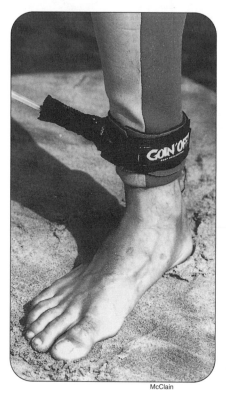
McClain

Leash
Make sure all the
knotted connections
aren't too mangled.
Strap the thing onto
your back ankle (the
back one after you
pop up). Make it snug,
not tight. The cord
should extend from
the outside of your
ankle.

OK. Now practice
walking into the water
without tripping on
your leash. Pretend
lots of people are
watching.

McClain

We Be Stylin'

There are a couple of things you should do in order to
look *sharp*. Carry your board under your arm with the
deck facing out and the nose pointed straight ahead.
Use one arm and one hand. Hold it in the middle.
Never drag your board. Make sure the leash is wrapped
neatly around the tail of the board and fastened down.
Don't let it trail behind you.

As you travel from your car to the beach and into the
water, walk with a strut. Back straight and chest puffed.
Speed can vary. A no-nonsense strutting jog is very
cool.

Once you've waded waist-deep into the ocean, you're

ready to plop yourself down and paddle out. Make sure you're in deep enough water. Scraping along in the shallows looks dorky. It's very important when you paddle that you keep your buns still. Actually, keep everything still except your arms. Keep your head up and look straight ahead.

When you make it outside, sit in the middle of your board, maybe a bit toward the back, so the nose points up. Face out to sea and sit up straight. Practice this by yourself and get it down. You won't be stylin' if you struggle just to sit on your surfboard without tipping over.

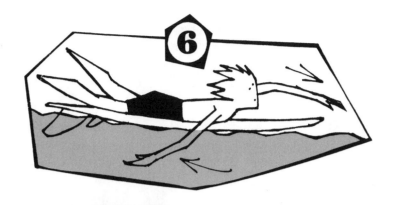

Paddling

Paddling is central to surfing. You'll spend most of your time paddling. It's how you get around and catch

Werner

waves. It's where the communication begins between you, the board, the water and ultimately, the wave.

Shoving Off
Wait for a lull (when the waves don't break). Point the board straight out in waist-deep water, plop yourself on your board and paddle like you're swimming the crawl stroke. That is, while one arm is digging and thrusting, the other is reaching. You'll find out real quick if you're in trim (balanced on the board). Too far forward ... you'll pearl or nose dive. Too far back ...

McClain

Wading out — Simple enough if you point the board directly into the surf and begin paddling when the water is waist-deep.

This is **bad paddling form**. Dave is too far forward. Christine is too far back.

McClain

McClain

This is **perfect form**. The nose of the board is just clearing the surface. Christine is centered, her head is up and she's looking straight ahead. She paddles with an even, hand-over-hand stroke.

Paddling out in good trim.

Still inside the impact zone, she prepares to deal with a wave.

The wave is breaking in front of Christine. Her board is pointed straight into the white water. She pushes herself up slightly so that the white water can pass around her more easily.

She gets pushed back, but because she's headed straight into the wave, she doesn't get rolled. She's got a good grip on her surfboard.

Christine immediately positions herself back into trim ...

... and paddles hard to regain her forward momentum.

you'll stall. Wiggle front or back to gain trim, always making sure the board is pointed straight out toward the waves.

Meet any white water straight on. This allows the least resistance to the wave. You'll be pushed back, but not rolled. When in doubt, paddle, paddle, paddle straight out! Do not wipe your eyes, fiddle with your hair or pull up your swim suit until you've made it outside (beyond the breaking waves). And don't be a crybaby. If you get washed inside, wait for another lull and try, try, try again! But seriously, if the surf is too consistent and strong, hang it up. Don't struggle. Wait for smaller waves.

I Made It!

Once outside, just practice paddling. Get used to your surfboard. Find the trim and work on your stroke. If the board doesn't float you or paddle easily, now is the time to take it back and try another. Don't struggle with a board that doesn't work for you.

If all is well, cruise around for a while. This is how the world looks and feels out here. Check it all out. Take your time. Remember, paddling is what gets you out, into a wave and out of trouble. Become confident with your paddling before you do anything else.

Being Afraid of Waves

I know people who show no fear of surf no matter how big. I'm not exactly one of those. What I do is deal with it and paddle out anyway. Actually, I'm more afraid of doing headers and embarrassing myself than I am of the physical danger of wiping out. That's vanity for you.

Fear is hard to distinguish from excitement sometimes. And sometimes they blend. You want to be excited about surfing, and it's OK to be a little frightened as long as you don't flip out or freeze. Waves won't hurt you (at least the kind you should be in) if you keep a thing or two in mind.

The most powerful act of the wave is its tumbling down when it breaks. Avoid having the wave break right on top of you. You won't get hurt (in small surf) but you will plunge down, spin around and get knocked off your board. Actually, all this is not necessarily un-fun, it just impedes your surfing.

Remember, waves are meant to be fun and exciting. There's a natural course of events on a given day of surfing. Be less afraid and more aware of what the conditions are and dealing with them won't be such a frightful struggle.

You'll <u>never</u> forget the first time.

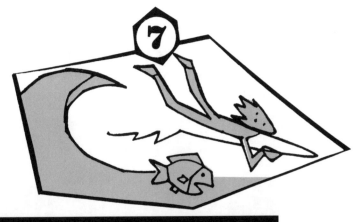

Catching a Wave

Full throttle moments in my life include turning a triple play in Little League, being accepted into an illustration program in college, receiving my first check as an independent businessman, getting married and holding our daughter for the first time. My first wave fits in there, too. In fact, after 25 years of surfing and countless waves, I remember that wave as much as any.

And it was hardly a wave at all. Indian River Inlet, Delaware. Summer of 1963. The surf was hardly surging onto the beach. The swells rolled up and sort of lapped the sand. I don't remember them even breaking. My best friend and I rented surfboards, courtesy of my uncle, and plunged in. I remember paddling into the swell ... and then it happened.

For me (and countless surfers), catching that first wave was a miracle. Feeling the wave take you is one of those "this is it" moments we all have a handful of in a lifetime. I stood up and immediately rammed into the sand — my buddy screaming, "Hang Ten!" as my head swam in adrenaline. Although the ride lasted less than a hiccup, the memory remains. And continues to be a strong reminder of what it's all about: Pure, unadulterated **stoke** (joy!).

Not having caught the wave, Dave stands up too soon and **stalls out.** He should have paddled a stroke or two more.

Paddling Into Your First Wave

The best way to learn is to catch the swell before the wave breaks. Don't mess around with the white water. Catching the swell is where it all begins in surfing, not bashing around in the soup (white water).

You'll learn in time where to position yourself in order to catch waves, but for now check out where everyone else is sitting and waiting. This is called the lineup.

Paddle into the wave the same way you have been paddling — hand over hand until you feel yourself being taken. It's unmistakable. Make sure you're in trim. If you catch the wave correctly, you'll slide down the face nicely. If you're too far forward, you'll

Pearling, or nose-diving because weight is too far forward.

Werner

pearl. Too far back, you'll stall — either out of the wave or you'll hang up on top and do a header (free fall over).

Get this part down — catching a wave without pearling or stalling. If you do it right, you'll shoot out fast, a bit in front of the breaking wave, then get caught by the soup and zip toward shore. You may just want to do this for a while without attempting to stand. Stay on your belly and get a feel for the interaction between you, the board and the wave.

Christine paddles into a swell, maintaining proper trim.

McClain

She has caught the swell. The board is sliding down the face of the wave. This is called **dropping in**.

In order not to pearl, or nose-dive, Christine pushes herself up and shifts her weight back.

Shooting In.

Stop!
Are you having fun? If not, check it out:

1. Is the board manageable? If not, get one that is, NOW.

2. Is the surf too big or powerful? If so, come back another day or find a gentler spot.

3. Are your paddling skills awkward? If so, practice some more.

4. Are you pointing the board straight into the white water when you're inside? If not, you're getting killed.

5. Are you paddling hard to get back outside? You cannot take coffee breaks inside. Move quickly out of the impact zone. Yes, I know. It's a lot of work!

Surfing should be fun all the time. That's what it's there for. Make sure you take the proper steps to ensure just that.

I'm Standing Up!
Standing up is like riding a bike without training wheels for the first time — when Dad let go and you peddled on your own down the street. You did what you may have thought impossible. Learning to drive a stick is sort of like that, too. Going from your belly to your feet on a speeding wave will probably seem even more daunting — **But you can do it!**

When you get good at catching the swell, try popping up as soon as the wave takes you. Don't hesitate. Don't

Paddling into the swell.

Having caught the swell, Christine begins her pop-up.

Note how trim is maintained. More pix next page.

Standing up in an athletic crouch. Feet are shoulder-width and her center of gravity is low.

Riding the wave straight into the beach is called "straight-off Adolph"!

hop on your knees. Don't wait to slide down to the bottom. Do it when you **feel** it. Disregard thoughts of grace, style, timing or "what ifs." Pop up like you did on the beach. Don't think, just do.

And Bingo! You'll be standing! Oh my Lordy! You'll actually be standing! And then you'll fall off.

Cover your head and make sure you fall away from the board. Lean into your fall and you'll just get wet. If the leash tugs, you'll know the board is away from you. No tug, watch it. Don't resurface without your hands over your head in case the board is above you.

Wiggle your fanny back onto your board, head back out and do it again and again and again. But of course, you shouldn't need to coach yourself at this point. Because you stood up and you're so pumped, you'll hope the whole beach was watching!

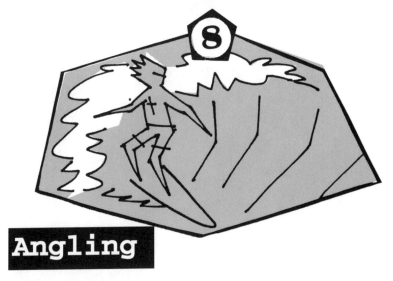

Angling

Going Sideways

Look at the waves at your break or in the surfing magazines. Look at the surfers. Notice how they're going sideways, either right or left, away from the breaking part of the wave. This, in its broadest sense, is called angling. As opposed to going straight into shore, like you have been doing (straight-off Adolph).

Are You Popping Up?

Angling is your next challenge after you've mastered paddling, taking off on a swell, and standing up before the swell breaks. If you've been standing up only after sliding down the wave, you must learn how to drop in and pop up right away.

Let's Do It!

As you paddle for a wave, begin by angling in the same direction the wave is breaking. If the wave is breaking left, angle left. If the wave is breaking right, angle right. As the wave picks you up, pop up as before and aim the board ahead of the curl, or the breaking part of the wave. Keep your board in trim and steer by leaning. Taking off at an angle should eliminate the need to turn the board for now.

Putting it all together — Paddling into the swell at an angle.

Popping up, maintaining the angle.

Up and Away. Dave is racing away from curl, or the breaking part of the wave.

Dave is demonstrating perfect trim. The nose of the board is just inches above the surface. Note his stance, position of feet and slight crouch.

When you start angling — seeing and feeling how the board speeds along the swell, you'll discover a thrill as great as standing up for the first time. Tearing along in front of the break, with the wall of the wave forming in front of you, is the real thing. This is where you'll be truly stoked or not at all. If this doesn't curl your hairs, you're destined to be a bean counter. You won't or don't like sex, chocolate or puppies, either.

Angling is at the heart of all those maneuvers you see done so effortlessly by expert surfers. It's the essence of the wave-riding experience. It's my hope, and the goal of this book, to get you out there first of all, standing up and finally angling along the peaking swell. You may never need to go beyond that to experience the magic of surfing. You'll only need more and more waves.

Early Stoke

For my fifteenth birthday, I wanted to go surfing. This was significant because: a) I lived in Dover, Delaware — fifty miles from the Indian River Inlet, the closest surf spot to my home. b) My birthday is December 11 and on that day, it was snowing. c) The only wet suit I had was a short john. This suit had no coverage on arms or legs and very little over the chest. d) I was too young to drive.

My parents drove me to the beach and huddled in the station wagon as I plunged into the 45-degree Atlantic ocean. I think the surf was one foot and choppy. I don't remember much. I think my brain cells froze on impact with the first wave I paddled through. I didn't stay out long.

I do remember staggering back across the icy beach and hurling myself into the back of the station wagon with my board. And damn near in agony from the cold. Mom threw a blanket over me and we drove home. I couldn't get out of the wetsuit. I couldn't move my fingers to try. I just chattered back there with the car heater on full blast.

Crazy? Absolutely. But determined to try. Give it all you got as you learn. The returns are enormous.

Waves

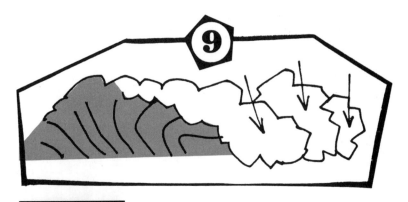

Waves

Waves are extraordinary things. Beautiful, fascinating, ever-changing. Powered by an undeniable, un-seen force. Nature's masterpieces. Once beyond the physical act of paddling and standing, the rest is riding your imagination as well as the wave. The mind tends to blur the distinction.

A Simple Explanation
Waves are the end result of a very long, sweeping journey. Hundreds, even thousands of miles away, strong, steady winds blow across the ocean's surface, raising ripples and chop. These winds are so consistent and cover such a large area, that the chop turns into what is called a "sea." With a life of its own, the sea races downwind from its origin, and organizes itself into vast lines of swell that march across the ocean's expanse. As swells near the shore and shallow water, they peak into waves and spill over or break.

Wave Shapes
The swell is very much affected by the bottom of the

A spilling, beach break wave.

A top-to-bottom and tubing, beach break wave.

shallows along a given coastline, as well as by the shape and curve of the shore.

A beach with a long and gradual rise from deep water to shore will encourage the swells to form spilling waves. As discussed in Chapter Two, these waves crumble down their faces. Perfect for kooks like you.

An abrupt change from deep to shallow water causes the swells to peak quicker and pitch their crests as opposed to just toppling over. An extreme form of this type of wave is the "tube" always glorified by magazines, television, videos and movies.

Of course, a lot of other things influence waves besides the bottom. Local winds blowing side to side (sideshore) or from the ocean (onshore), tend to blow out surf (make it bumpy). Winds blowing into the surf (offshore) can enhance the shape of the wave. Kelp can counter the effects of the wind, although it slows the waves down. Various currents, especially riptides, can tear up the surf. Tides make dramatic changes in the surf because they alter the depth along the shore. Every spot has its own set of variables. You will be wise to know what they are at your surfing area.

Types of Breaks

Beach breaks have sandbars that cause waves to break. Sandbars change a lot from season to season, month to month and even day to day.

Reef breaks have a rock or coral bottom that tends to standardize the condition of the breaking waves. It usually breaks in the same spot.

Down the line — This very ridable wave is peeling along its length in a uniform fashion.

This rider is facing a **section** — a part of a wave that breaks ahead of the initial peak.

McClain

Closed-out — This wave is breaking along its entire length at the same time. Angling along the swell is impossible.

Point breaks are points of land on the shoreline that approaching swells wrap around and break over as portions of the wave's length near the shallower water. This is also a more predictable break than a beach break.

So What Makes for a Good Surf Spot?

Waves break up and down a coastline. Yet not every portion of the coast has good surfing waves. Surfers need waves that break from an initial peak and peel off in one or two directions. That is, the wave begins to break sooner at one section of its length and continues to peel and break in a gradual fashion from that peak.

Closed-out surf are waves that break along their length at the same time or in such large, irregular sections that angling along the swell is impossible — you can only go straight. And that's not where we're headed with this surfing business. At first, going straight is fine, but the real thrill of surfing is riding that unbroken swell down the line.

Surfing Hot Spots

The January 1985 issue of *Surfer Magazine* furnished a partial list of the world's best surf spots:

Jeffrey's Bay, South Africa
Nias, Indonesia
Rincon, California
Malibu, California
Pipeline, Hawaii
Oxnard, California
Shark Island, Australia
North Narrabeen, Australia
Blacks, California
Moorea, Tahiti
Rocky Point, Hawaii
Off the Wall, Hawaii
Black Rock, Australia
Padang Padang, Indonesia
Puerto Escondido, Mexico
Sunset Beach, Hawaii
Pupukea, Hawaii
Maalaea, Hawaii
Newport Wedge, California
Burleigh Heads, Australia
Cave Rock, South Africa
Honolua Bay, Hawaii
The Bluff, West Australia
Lower Trestles, California
Backdoor, Hawaii

In fairness, I'd like to add these spots from the east

These are tubes or barrels. Every surfer's dream is fitting inside one. Christine on top and Dave below.

coast, USA:

Montauk Point, New York
Cape Hatteras, North Carolina
Sebastian Inlet, Florida

Twenty-eight spots don't make a complete list. Great waves are breaking right now in 1,001 places around the globe not mentioned here.

Think about *that*.

Crowds, Localism & You

A part of me thinks this is nuts. Writing a how-to-surf guide may encourage more people to surf and none of us want that. The waves are crowded enough. But it's doubtful that this guide will seriously affect the size of the surfing world. I do hope it helps new surfers who read it to learn correctly and safely.

And I say this to those who do: Have respect.

Good Old Days
In the '50s, when surfing was practiced by the hardy few, there were plenty of waves for everyone. Everybody knew each other on a given stretch of coast-line. Surfers were truly a brotherhood — as only a fanatical few can be who practice any activity outside the mainstream.

The '60s popularized surfing. You saw it in magazines, at the movies and heard it on the radio. With all that came the inevitable crowds. You may have heard about the surfing brotherhood of that era. OK, maybe a bit of that feeling was around, but really — how could you feel like a brother to 400,000 surfers?

Localism: A Surfer's Government

Surfers began to band together locally and made it tough for outsiders to surf at their spot. This is localism. It's still here and here to stay. Usually, it's just a vibe in the water — you are definitely not welcome. Locals take off on you and somebody will yell at you at least once. Fights happen, but not nearly as often as legend or rumor has it.

Now this sounds grim, I know. However, all the localism I've ever dealt with is really quite manageable if you follow a few golden rules. And despite the bad press, localism isn't a bad thing nowadays. On a crowded coastline, it's the only way to get waves. The only thing better is no crowds, and for most of us, those days are gone unless you travel.

Localism at its best is a form of government. The people who have consistently surfed at a given spot for some time and have been accepted by the local crew for displaying a good attitude and a certain level of competence will get waves. It's that simple. This you have to accept. You have some dues to pay to get waves.

Have Respect

As you begin surfing and desire more and more waves of quality, you're going to have to develop an attitude. You see, in the surfing world no one cares about your status. Everything you get will have to be earned in the water. You have no right to waves. You will have to make other surfers respect you, and to do that, you must show respect first.

Know Yourself
You're a beginner, so stay away from the experts. You're lousy, so you must surf lousy areas on the fringe of a surf spot. As you become better, you can think about competing for the better waves. But first ...

Know the Locals
Take note of who surfs every day at your spot (or spots). Who gets the waves? These are the people who you want to know. These are the people you want to have know you.

Stay Focused. Keep Cool.
Let your face become known. Surf as much as you can, and stay out of the locals' way. If you get snaked, let it go. If you get yelled at, let it go. Become a fixture out there. Show that you can take it. That will be your ultimate strength. If you get into a fight with an established local at this point, it will be like a politician getting caught taking a bribe or poking some bimbo. You may never live it down.

This is the hardest part. Being ignored, getting snaked, having some bullet-brain call you names and getting very few waves. It's a real bummer, but you can take it. Over time it will improve.

Eventually you'll share friendly words with one of the locals. Maybe he or she has the same job, interests, or major in school as you. This is called making friends. This is also being smart. If one of them thinks you're

OK, you're on your way. Take it slow and easy. Try to be friendly without displaying too much of the desperation you feel. It's all part of the game.

If all this seems beneath you, try going out there without diplomacy. Try going out there with the attitude "Hey, these waves don't belong to anybody. Here I am, take it or leave it!"

Perhaps you've become quite skilled and you've noticed that you surf better than some of the locals. "Hey, I'm good and you're not! Out of my way!" Go ahead. Write me your success story. Please. I'll include it in the next reprint. Fat chance.

Instead, have patience, wear a smile and use your brains. One morning you'll find yourself in the lineup as a local. You'll have friends. You'll get waves. And you'll pity all the newcomers who come and go with tire marks on their backs because they didn't show respect.

Anarchy: Surfing's Future?
If you still think localism is a bad thing, check out those spots that have evolved beyond mere localism. These are the legendary spots of the surfing world. In California, there's Rincon, Malibu and Trestles. In Hawaii, it's any of a dozen spots on the north shore of Oahu. Every coastline in the world has its premiere break. Welcome to the international free zones! Everybody takes off, all the time. The lineups are bobbing carpets of surfers. Getting waves is like playing Lotto.

Localism really doesn't work at these places anymore because of the sheer numbers. No, I'll take my chances at those spots that suffer only a hostile home team. You can work yourself into any lineup, if it's still a lineup. In gridlock, you're just another stalled vehicle.

The next wave is <u>mine!</u>

Brotherhood

There was a time when all surfboards were so big they were usually strapped on top of the vehicle. As you traveled up or down the coast anybody could see you were a surfer. When surfers approached each other from opposite directions, it was customary to signal to the other with an up or down turn of the thumb to indicate what the surf was like from whence each came. This courtesy was always given enthusiastically and truthfully. If the thumbs down signal was given, the receiver of this message would stop and turn around. Why waste the gas?

This was universal trust. I can imagine signaling to surfers these days. They'd think you were flashing some sort of gang sign and run you into a ditch.

What Now?

Buying a Board
The rentals you've been floundering on have given you a vague idea of what you need. Buy a board that comes as close to that as possible. You don't have to buy new. Again, don't look for beauty. Get a board that works for as cheap as possible.

Big Boards / Small Boards
In general, there are three sizes of boards. A board is usually considered a short board if it's seven feet in length or shorter. A board is considered a longboard if it's nine feet long or longer. In between are what some call fun boards, which for the most part, ride like a short board with a greater planing surface.

When you go into a surf shop, you'll probably see a lot of boards under seven feet and a few boards quite a bit longer. These longboards were the norm before 1965. A typical length back then was 9'6". When it was discovered that you could successfully ride smaller boards, short boards swept the sport like nothing else ever did.

McClain

Longboard and short board – Vehicles that provide two different ways to ride the waves.

Longboard stylings ...

McClain

Shorter boards allow you to stand in one spot and maneuver by shifting weight. They're more maneuverable than longboards because they're lighter, thinner and have a tighter turn radius. Short boards are the overwhelming choice of surfers everywhere, although longboard surfing has made a dramatic comeback in recent years.

Longboard surfing demands footwork. One has to walk around on a longboard to maneuver and trim because of all the length. It's a different style of surfing. Since it requires so much footwork and the maneuvers are so drawn out, longboard surfing can be quite graceful. Longboards also have the advantage of being able to paddle faster and catch waves sooner, due to the greater planing surface.

Both boards and styles, of course, are legitimate. Watch who surfs what, and check out what you like. Maybe you'll learn how to surf both. You should!

Learning New Stuff
Surf with the best surfers you can find (just stay out of their way). As in any pursuit, expertise rubs off. Study their feats and keep at it!

Surfer Magazine has run a series of how-to articles on advanced techniques called: Surfer Tips and Expert Advice. For more information write:

Surfer
Editorial Staff
PO Box 1028
Dana Point, CA 92629

Short board maneuverability.

Have Fun. Have Respect.
Surfing is one of the things that life should be about.
We all have to worry about money, jobs or school, dogs
or kids, etc. But there really should be something else.
Something more. Something pure that can be taken as
is without thought to yesterday or tomorrow.

When I go surfing, I know I haven't wasted my time.
I've involved myself with something that's *as good as
it gets.* Living is very much worthwhile if I can go
surfing every day.

So enjoy the experience and try to get along with
other surfers. After all, most of them feel like you.
Carry yourself with respect and give it back.

Have fun.

A Little History

Children of the Sea
The first surfer was a Polynesian.

Going way back (before 1400), a migration of
Caucasians headed east across Asia (from India), inter-
married with Oriental and Malaysian folks along the
way and made little brown, almond-eyed babies. These
pre-Polynesians sat on the beach someplace in
Southeast Asia, gazing at the open ocean and, unlike
practically any other people in history, decided home-
sweet-home was out **there** somewhere.

Loading up the kids, some animals and their favorite
plants, they set sail in canoes for parts unknown. No
map. No compass. In little, eeny boats. From island to
island speck, they wandered eastward to Tahiti. Living
off the ocean and obviously in some sort of special
harmony with the wind, the currents and the stars.
These people did not lack optimism, assertion or self-
confidence.

Tahiti was nice, of course, but a few of our Polynesian ancestors thought it might be cool to make a trip north. Like 2,000 miles worth. No compass. No map. In those eeny boats. They did and ran into Hawaii.

Now it's time to look at a map. Find Hawaii. Now find Tahiti. Your best friend wants you and he to sail from there to there in his new Hobie Cat. You'll bring some water and some food, but hey, you can just fish on the way and catch rain water. No map. No compass. No radio. Just the stars. Sounds like a real treat, right? Well, these folks did something like that at least 500 years ago and didn't even know where they were going!

These Polynesians were at home in the water. It fed them, amused them and gave them faith. It was in their blood. They got to know the ocean like their European counterparts got to know the land. It's only natural to assume that this race of people were the first to surf.

And surf they did. In rituals, contests and just for fun. Songs, chants, and dances reveal the importance of wave riding in the Polynesian culture. There were special months to surf, special prayers for surf and special rules to surf by. And everybody surfed. Royalty as well as the rest (even though the king had his own spot, forbidden to everyone else on penalty of death). It really was a surfer's paradise until ...

The Dark Age
Cap'n Cook and crew were the first white men to lay eyes on surfers. In 1777, the English explorer saw a canoeist in Tahiti ride a huge swell into the beach. He was stoked: "I could not help concluding that this man

felt the most supreme pleasure while he was driven on so fast and smoothly by the sea." Later, during the same voyage, he discovered the Hawaiian Islands.

Returning to the big island of Hawaii in 1779, a member of the crew recorded the first account of surfers riding the waves on boards: "The boldness and address with which they performed was altogether astonishing."

But the white guys didn't paddle out. Actually, most Euroweenies didn't swim at the time. Not even sailors. Swimming for fun was not only considered uncool, but very unhealthy. This pitiful, misguided concept almost proved fatal for the sport.

Westerners soon came to stay and, of course, to change and control things *their* way. Their most significant import was disease, which nearly wiped out the native population. Attitudes about religion and making money forever bent the culture that loved the sea. Somehow the missionaries convinced the Hawaiian queen that many aspects of the island lifestyle were bad, including surfing, and had them banned.

So began the dark age of surfing. A period of almost 100 years when surfing practically disappeared.

From the Ashes
By the turn of the century, surfing's ungodly, immoral and frivolous branding began to fade. The exploits of a small number of pioneers helped turn the tide. The following individuals all began their surfing careers at Waikiki Beach, Honolulu. There the sport had been

kept alive throughout the bleak 19th century, and had become something of an attraction, due to the surfing exploits of the original Beach Boys who surfed there.

George Freeth
Of Irish and Hawaiian descent, Freeth is probably best remembered as the surfer who first brought the sport to the mainland. In 1907, he was hired by a railroad company to perform his surfing skills in Redondo Beach, California, in order to attract customers. His exhibitions thrilled thousands. But more importantly, he taught the first Californians how to ride waves.

Alexander Hume Ford
Ford taught Jack London how to surf in 1907. London was one of the most popular writers of his time and was so taken by surfing that he wrote magazine articles about it and included the sport in his books. This is like getting exposure on the Oprah Show today.

In 1910, he founded the Outrigger Canoe Club at Waikiki. Its stated purpose was to advance "the almost forgotten art of surfriding ... "

Duke Kahanamoku
Duke is considered the father of the modern era of surfing. A full-blooded Polynesian and a surfer since childhood, he became an international celebrity by setting world records in the 100-yard and 100-meter freestyle swimming events. He won gold medals in those events in the 1912 and 1920 Olympics.

Duke barnstormed the mainland, captivating the crowds with his surfing prowess in California, New

Grannis Collection

It's 1946 in Palos Verdes, California. LeRoy Grannis poses with his handcrafted redwood and balsa surfboard. The board is over 11 feet long and weighs 65 pounds.

Doc Ball rides one of Tom Blake's hollow "cigar boxes" *circa* 1940. Wetsuits weren't around yet. It's called grinning and bearing it.

York and New Jersey. He was the first to surf the east coast and introduced the sport to Australia as well. Kahanamoku went on to make Hollywood movies and became ambassador-at-large for Hawaii and the sport of surfing. Duke was elected Sheriff of Honolulu and held the post for 26 years. At the time of his death in 1968, he was legend.

California Innovations
The first half of the 20th century saw a steady growth in surfing's popularity. California became the epicenter for surfboard innovation and design. It was here that the seed of its future popularity was planted.

Tom Blake
It can be said that Blake was the first serious surfboard designer to come around in 500 years. Until 1926, surfboards had been made out of wood — preferably redwood. The boards were big and heavy — up to 150 pounds! They had no fin and maneuvering them was practically impossible.

Blake built the first hollow board in 1926 and the so-called "cigar boxes" were the norm for another 20 years. He got the weight down to 40–50 pounds, and in 1935, attached the first fin to a board. His other important firsts include writing the first book about surfing, *Hawaiian Surfboard* (1935), and first to surf Malibu in 1926.

Bob Simmons
In 1949 another Californian, Bob Simmons, built a board from styrofoam sandwiched between plywood and sealed with resin and fiberglass. Later, he added

balsa rails. These were the first boards to be commer-
cially successful. They were relatively light, easily trans-
portable and maneuverable. They were the prototypes
for the modern era, and along with balsa boards, were
the rage for almost 10 years.

The Blank = Modern Surfing

In 1958 Hobie Alter and Gordon Clark came up with
the first urethane "blank," or foam core, for a surfboard.
This type of foam could be shaped easily in endless
variations. Once coated with resin and fiberglass, the
board became the lightest, most maneuverable wave
tool ever created. This opened the door to better and
higher performance surfing. The materials and methods
of construction are basically the same to this day.

By 1960, history and technology slam-banged together
to make surfing a huge fad. The boards were smaller,
lighter, easier to manage and more affordable than ever
before. The population in Southern California was
exploding. Music, movies and clothing celebrated the
"coastline craze." Surfing became mainstream in a very
big way. California was the capital, but surfing also blos-
somed in Australia and the eastern United States. The
beach had gradually become a popular point of interest
throughout the century, but in 1960 it was the place to
be and surfing was its ultimate expression.

Small Boards and Big Moves

Boards got short, then shorter by the end of the sixties.
It was discovered you could still surf and stand on a
board one foot, two feet, even three or four feet less in
length than previously thought. The small, light boards
enabled surfers to achieve ever more radical ways to

Duke Kahanamoku – What can you say about a man that almost single-handedly put surfing on the world map? Before him, no one surfed California, the eastern United States or Australia. Duke went to these places on his surfing tours and forever changed the way the world looked at waves.

Grannis Collection

Iron Man – LeRoy Grannis at Sunset Beach, Hawaii in 1962. He was pushing 50 when this photo was taken. Thirty years later, he's still at it.

ride the waves. New board and fin designs continue to take them even further.

Surfing in the last 20 years has grown worldwide and world-class. Top surfers are among the world's elite athletes. Surfboard design makes the space program envious. And people just can't get enough of it. If they don't have a coastline, they'll build a wave pool and stand in line.

What began as an ancient sport of island kings has evolved into a sport for all nations and all people. The fad became a pastime, became a sport and has become a fixture of coastlines everywhere. Surviving persecution, commercialism, silly trends and the fears of people who never tried, surfing will always be around. And always cherished. By the bold, the young at heart and the lovers of life.

Champion tandem surfers Pat and Lynne Weber are the owners of San Diego Surfing Academy.

San Diego's
Surfing Coach

Pat and Lynne Weber's San Diego Surfing Academy has taught more than 2,000 people how to surf since 1995. The youngest student has been 6 and the oldest 61. Pat rode his first wave in 1966, and has been competing since he was 12. He and wife Lynne have won nine tandem surfing titles.

Pat's interview provides a glimpse of what you're in for and answers a lot of commonly asked questions.

How hard is it to learn to surf?
Surfing is *the* hardest sport to learn. Especially if you're an adult. That's because the medium, the ocean, is *dynamic.* The ocean is constantly changing. Strap on a pair of ice skates, the rink stays still. Strap on a pair of skis, the mountain remains static.

To become expert, surfing requires judgment and wave knowledge and that takes hundreds of hours in the water to acquire. Of course, a mentor or coach can supply a great deal of that knowledge and help you get started.

How long does it take to stand up?
You can stand in five minutes if you've been coached properly.

What are the stages leading to standing up?

It starts with a 15-minute beach lesson learning how to pop-up. How to stand in one smooth, crisp motion, using your hands as a fulcrum and your body as the lever. A surfer needs to *fire* up, *explode* into a pop-up.

They're so critical. Pop-ups are the most important thing about surfing. It's the threshold. It's the portal of the wave riding experience.

After the pop-ups on the beach, then what?

Say you've done it 20 times, even 50 times on the beach. It's not enough! When I was a kid learning to surf, I would spend the night popping up so I could get an edge on my friends. Because if you crawl to your feet, one knee at a time, you're not going to get the job done. Especially in critical waves.

There's a small window in which to stand. First you'll feel the lift of the wave, then you must paddle two or more strong strokes until you feel yourself descend that watery slope. That's when you fire up to your feet. If you miss it and ride on your belly all the way to the bottom of the swell, you'll have a "G" working against you. Instead of drawing 150 pounds to your feet, it will be 300!

After pop-ups what else is important?

I taught a young girl who had cerebral palsy. She charged 6-foot surf in order to learn. She was *determined*. Not technically perfect, but she *made* it happen.

Having said that, it helps to have natural balance. This sport is all about balance.

How do the learning curves compare between children and adults, boys and girls, men and women?

It's hard to generalize. I've had 9-year-old girls outperform their 14-year-old, all-star brothers because the girls had more control over their bodies. It doesn't hurt to have a sense of balance and a degree of athleticism, but that's not age- or gender-specific.

You don't care if they're 8 years old or 70?

No. At the Surfing Academy we try to match students with a board that floats them properly so that differences in size and strength play less of a part in the learning experience. It's important to have flotation in surfing equipment in order to paddle and catch waves easily.

As the surf grows in size, so does the importance of upper body strength. But since we teach our students at learning beaches, where the waves are suitable for beginners, there's less of a need for muscle.

What kind of physical requirements are there?

Bottom line: Be able to swim 500 yards without stopping. If you can do that you're in basic surfing condition. You can last a couple of hours without wilting. It's 25 yards across the pool. A lap is 50 yards. So that's 10 laps without stopping.

It's important to know that the board is not your flotation device! If the leash breaks you must know how to swim to save yourself.

What kind of surfboard should one learn on?

Sometimes pride gets in the way. You see the videos showing the top pros doing the tight turns and tail slides. It's like in any other sport when you see the top athletes taking it to the limit. The best make it look easy. You want enough flotation so that you can paddle and catch a wave, pop up to your feet, ride that wave and have fun.

Surfing is about the individual. It's about you. It's about what you get from it — your personal satisfaction. If you're not catching waves, if you're riding a board that's too short, too narrow or too thin, you're not catching waves and you're not having fun. It's all about having fun.

Surfing has grown up. If you showed up with a long-board in the '70s, you were ridiculed. Surfing was the exclusive domain of teenage boys. Girls were excluded. Older guys were excluded. Surfing has evolved. Today, anything goes. Young guys are riding '60s boards. Women are an important part of the sport. There's a supportive atmosphere. Surfing is a family thing.

If grandpa paddles out on a six-foot thruster, he's not going to get the job done. But if he uses a 10-foot-long, wide, thick, easy-to-paddle longboard, he's going to catch waves. He's going to be standing and he's going to be having a good time.

Don't let pride get in the way. It doesn't matter what you ride. It's not the arrow, it's the archer.

Is surfing dangerous?
Hell, yeah. I have the scars to prove it!

How do you minimize the dangers?
With a soft board. A soft board keeps it safe for those who don't have the ocean experience. Doyle soft boards will familiarize you with the sensations of surfing, paddling, catching the wave, getting to your feet and the thrill of riding nature's energy. They're made out of the same materials as a boogy board.

How important are lessons?
Surfing has never had teaching professionals like in

golf, tennis or skiing. Maybe that's because the numbers haven't been there to sustain the profession. But that's changing. More people are coming into the sport, including older people, who used coaching professionals when they learned how to sky dive, ocean dive, ski, whatever.

Learning how to surf used to be *just do it*! It was a rite of passage. But a teacher in any endeavor, on any level, shortens the learning curve. You can learn how to play piano by yourself, but you can learn more in an hour-lesson than in a month of plunking by yourself.

Instruction points you in the right direction. You might need one lesson, you might need a battery of lessons. Each student is different.

San Diego Surfing Academy provides surfing lessons, Baja surf trips and adult surf camps year round.

San Diego Surfing Academy
PO Box 99938
San Diego, CA 92169-1938
www.surfSDSA.com
1-800-447-SURF (7873)

Glossary

This is all you need to know plus a couple throwaways. English is still spoken and understood by most surfers in the USA so don't worry about the latest slang you may hear.

Angling: Going sideways or riding the wave along the unbroken portion of its length, ahead of the broken portion.

Beach Break: Where waves break over a sandbar.
Blown Out: Condition of waves torn up by wind.

Closed-out: Condition of waves that break all at once, making angling impossible.
Curl: Breaking part of a wave.

Dude: This word for "guy" has been around since 1972. It wasn't hip then, isn't hip now. Dudes are cowboy wannabees. Unfortunately, it has become a part of American culture. Or to be specific, a part of American mall culture.

Goofy Foot: As you stand on your surfboard, the natural preference for having your right foot forward.

Hang Ten: Placing all ten toes over the nose of a moving surfboard. Usually associated with longboard surfing.
Header: When you plunge down the face of a wave with the toppling crest.

Impact Zone: Where waves break.

Inside: The area "inside" the breaking waves. Also may refer to smaller waves breaking closer to shore or further in from an outside point of land.

Kook: Should be defined as an inexperienced or disrespectful surfer. It will come to mean anybody but you and your friends.

Lineup: That area outside the breaking waves where surfers sit on their boards and wait for waves.
Lip: The very tip of a cresting wave where it curls or plunges down.
Locals: Surfers who frequent a certain spot.
Localism: Rule by locals. Locals determine who gets waves and who does not. At best, it's a form of government and a relatively good one. At worst, it can be a cause for vandalism and bloodletting.
Lull: Waves arrive during certain periods of time. When they don't it's a lull.

Outside: The area "outside" the breaking waves. Also may refer to larger waves breaking further out from shore or a point of land.

Peak: That portion of the cresting swell that breaks first.
Pearl: When a moving surfboard nose-dives due to a rider's weight being too far forward.
Point Break: Where waves break around a point of land.
Pop-up: The almost singular motion of standing up on your surfboard, from belly to feet.

Reef Break: Where waves break over a reef.

Regular Foot: As you stand on your surfboard, the natural preference for having your left foot forward.

Rip: A current of water heading out to sea caused by strong surf.

Sea: Winds blowing strong and steady over a large area of water form chop and eventually a "sea." A sea in turn forms a swell.

Sets: The way waves arrive at a beach, with lulls in between.

Snaking: Catching a wave in front of another surfer who has caught the wave closer to the breaking part of the wave.

Soup: White water formed by a breaking wave.

Stall: When a moving surfboard slows due to a rider's weight being too far back.

Stick: A surfboard.

Swell: The marching lines of wind-inspired energy that travel across open water, crest and make waves in shallow water.

Trim: Being balanced fore and aft, and side to side on your surfboard, so as not to nose-dive or stall as you paddle or ride. Trim encourages maximum thrust through the water.

Tube: A type of wave that breaks top to bottom. The crest of the wave plunges out and down to the base of the wave, forming a hollow tube.

White Water: The broken or spent part of a wave that has peaked and toppled over. Also soup.

Wipe out: A fall off your surfboard.

Resources

SURF SHOPS

The best source for most everything *can* be a surf shop. There are about 1,000 nationwide with about the same number of owners. Surfers are very independent. There are few chains. Shops should be able to provide you with the best local information about:

Surfing areas
Conditions
Contests
Museums or historical displays
Organizations

Shops also provide:
Surfboards
Surfing gear
Surfers to talk to
Surfing magazines, newspapers and literature

MAGAZINES

In the USA, it's *Surfer* and *Surfing* magazines. It can be argued that these magazines used to hold the surfing world together — before money was being made and organizations became organized. They've always held a focus on hot spots, hot surfers, new maneuvers, contest results and surfing issues. Moreover, the magazines celebrate surfing in a razzle-dazzle, colorful, ultra-modern fashion, that tends to glorify the pursuit that we love. The market for *Surfer* and *Surfing* is the twenty-ish male who rides a short board.

For the ladies there's *SurferGirl*. Relatively new, the

magazine especially caters to the interests of female riders.

Since the modern era of surfing is middle-aged at this point, there are now surfing magazines for older surfers who may ride longboards. *Longboard* and *Surfers Journal* also cover hot spots, hot surfers and surfing issues, but tend to carry a bit more perspective and, of course, history. It should be noted that a lot of longboarders are younger people who are featured in these fine publications as well.

Longboard Magazine
110 East Palizada
Suite 301
San Clemente, CA 92672
949-366-8282

SurferGirl
PO Box 3618
Half Moon Bay, CA 94019
http://www.surfergrrl.com

Surfer Magazine
Surfer is one of the oldest and most revered *institutions* in modern surfing. It's commonly referred to as surfing's Bible.
PO Box 1028
Dana Point, CA 92629
714-496-5922
http://www.surfermag.com

Surfers Journal
Box 4006
San Clemente, CA 92672
http://www.surfersjournal.com

Surfing Magazine
950 Calle Amanecer
Suite C
San Clemente, CA 92672
714-492-7873

List of magazine sites on the Web
http://www.miningco.com
Click Sports/Water Sports/Surfing/Magazines

VIDEOS/MOVIES
Along our nation's shoreline, video stores (especially the major ones) carry surfing movies. These are usually tapes of hot surfers doing their thing with a contemporary sound track.

Among the very best introductions to surfing is Bruce Brown's film, *The Endless Summer*. Released in 1964, the movie manages to convey a very special feeling about surfing that still holds today. Thirty years later, Brown released *Endless Summer II,* which offers a fine update of where surfing is today.

Check out these Web sites:
http://miningco.com
Click Sports/Water Sports/Surfing/Videos

http://sur4.com
Click Industry/Videos

http://www.surfermag.com
Click Surf Shop/Videos

ORGANIZATIONS
Web sites:
Association of Surfing Professionals
http://www.asplive.com

Eastern Surfing Association
http://www.surfesa.org

National Scholastic Surfing Association
http://www.nssa.org

Surf Industry Manufacturers Association
http://www.sima.com

Surfer's Medical Association
http://www.damoon.net/sma/index.html

Surfrider Foundation
http://www.surfrider.org

Texas Gulf Surfing Association
http://www.questmp.com/surftgsa/index.html

United States Surfing Federation (western region)
http://www.surfergrrl.com/am/ussf/west/index.html

List of organizations on the Web
http://www.miningco.com
Click Sports/Water Sports/Surfing/Organizations

MUSEUMS
California Surf Museum
223 North Coast Highway
Oceanside, CA 92054
760-721-6876
http://www.surfmuseum.org

International Surfing Museum
411 Olive Avenue
Huntington Beach, CA 92648
714-960-3483
http://www.surfingmuseum.org

The Santa Cruz Surfing Museum
Mark Abbott Memorial Lighthouse
West Cliff Drive, Santa Cruz, CA
Mail: 1305 East Cliff Drive
Santa Cruz, CA 95062
408-429-3429
http://www.cruzio.com/~scva/surf.html

Surfworld Museum (Australia)
Beach Road Torquay
Victoria 3228 Australia
+61-03-5261-4606
http://www.surfworld.org.au

RESOURCES ON THE WEB
The following sites offer extensive information about surfing conditions, other links, history, organizations and gear. A great place to start.

http://www.real-surfing.com (Australia)

http://www.miningco.com
Click Sports/Water Sports/Surfing

http://www.sur4.com

http://www.surfinfo.com

http://www.surfinfo.com.au (Australia)

http://www.surflink.com

http://www.surfvideo.com

SURF REPORTS
See also "RESOURCES ON THE WEB"

http://www.surfcheck.com
California and Baja

http://www.surfinfo.com
East coast surf check and information center

http://www.surfline.com
Hawaii, California, Florida and Costa Rica

The Surf Report: Journal of Worldwide Surfing Destinations
Surfer Magazine
PO Box 1028
Dana Point, CA 92629
or
http://www.surfermag.com
Click Surf Shop/Surf Report

BOOKS
amazon.com's list of surfing books
http://www.amazon.com
Click Browse Subjects/ Sports and Outdoors/
Water Sports/Surfing

Top Ten Sellers (amazon.com as of 2-99)

Caught Inside:A Surfer's Year on the California Coast
Daniel Duane/ North Point Press/ 1997

*Longboarder's Start-Up:A Guide to Longboard
Surfing*
Doug Werner/ Tracks Publishing/ 1996

Jaws Maui
Blue Max, Lyons/ Jaws Maui Ltd/ 1997

Surfriders: In Search of the Perfect Wave
Matt Warshaw, Ed M. Warshaw/ Collins Publishing San
Francisco/ 1997

Learn to Surf
James MacLaren
The Lyons Press/ 1997

Surfing San Onofre to Point Dume: 1936-1942
Don James, Donald H. James/ Chronicle Books/ 1998

*Surfer's Start-Up:A Beginner's Guide to Surfing
(second edition)*
Doug Werner/ Tracks Publishing/ 1999

Surfing:A History of the Ancient Hawaiian Sport
James D. Houston, Ben R. Surfin Finney/ Pomegranate/
1996

Surfers: Photographs by Patrick Cariou
Patrick Cariou/ Power House Cultural Entertainment/
1997

The Surfer's Guide to Florida
Amy Vansnat/ Pineapple Press/ 1998

GEAR
Surfboards
There are a number of fine, established surfboard man-ufacturers in the industry. However, there are scores of lesser known names that surfers swear by. Actually each region has its favorites. There will be prominent local brands in your area.

Here's the thing: Surfboards are still shaped and glassed by hand. It's most definitely a craft, and in the hands of the best, an art. When you want your very own board, seek out a shaper in your area and discuss it with him face to face. Of course, you can buy off the rack, but it's great to develop a relationship with a master shaper who knows how you surf.

Wetsuits
Wetsuits are a different story. They're manufactured like clothing and seldom custom made because there is little need. Buy a brand name through a shop in your area where you can be fitted.

Here are some good names:
Aleeda
Billabong
Body Glove
Hotline
O'Neill
Quicksilver

Sites on the Web that carry gear information
http://miningco.com
Click Sports/Water Sports/Surfing/Boards, Wax & More

http://sur4.com
Click Industry

TELEVISION
Surfing programs lurk here and there on the tube.

H3O: Hawaiian Heavy Water
http://www.h3o.com

Liquid Stage: The Lure of Surfing
KPBS TV San Diego
http://facs.scripps.edu/surf/lstage.html

Radical Side TV Show (Florida)
http://www.radicalside.com

Bibliography

Kampion, Drew. The Book of Waves. Santa Barbara, Calif.: Arpel Graphics, Inc., and Surfer Publications, 1989.

Klein, H. Arthur. Surfing. New York: J.B. Lippincott Company, 1965.

Surfer Magazine. San Juan Capistrano, Calif.: Surfer Publications, Inc.

Surfing Magazine. San Clemente, Calif.: Western Empire Publications, Inc.

Wardlaw, Lee. Cowabunga! The Complete Book of Surfing. New York: Avon Books, 1991.

Wright, Bank. Surfing California. Redondo Beach, Calif.: Manana Publishing, 1973.

Index

Alter, Hobie 98
Angling 65-68

Beach break 73
Blake, Tom 96, 97
Blank, urethane 98
Board control 29-30
Breaks, types of 73-74
Buying a board 85

Cairns, Ian 9
Captain Cook 92, 93
Catching waves 54-63
Challenge (difficulty) of surfing 103
Clark, Gordon 98
Closed-out surf 75

Dangers of surfing 107
Dark age of surfing 92-93
Dick and Jane 9

Euroweenies 93
Etiquette (Rules of the Road) 35-39
        concerning cutting off (snaking) 36-39
        in the lineup 36
        when paddling out 35-36
        when taking off 39

Gear 15-22
Gillard, Christine 13
Goofy foot 41
Grannis, LeRoy 10, 11, 95, 100

Fear 52-53
Freeth, George 94

History 91-101
Hume, Alexander Ford 94

Interview, Pat Weber 103-108

Kahanamoku, Duke 94, 96, 99
Killer board 30

Learning curves 105
Learning new stuff (*Surfer* Tips) 88
Leash 20, 44
Library Journal 9
Lobster traps 32
Localism 79-84
Longboards 85, 86, 87, 88

Montalbano, David 13

Paddling 47-53
     form 49
Pearling 57
Physical requirements 105
Point break 75
Pop-ups 40-43, 104-105
Proning 58-59
Racks 20
Reef break 73
Regular foot 41
Riptides 32-33

Safety 29-34

San Diego Surfing Academy 103, 108
Section 74
Sex 13
Short boards 85, 86, 88, 89, 98, 100

Simmons, Bob 97-98
Soft (beginner) boards 15-16, 107

Spilling wave 25, 72
Sponge 15-16
Surfing instruction 107-108
Stalling 56
Standing up 60-63, 103-104
Straight-off Adolph 62
Stylin' 45-46
Surf spots 23-24, 75, 76, 78
        world's best surf spots 76, 78
Surfboards 14-19, 106-107

Top-to-bottom wave 25, 72
Tubes (barrels) 77

Waves 70-78
        origin 71
        shapes 71-73
Waves, proper surfing ("right") waves 23-27
Wax 20
Waxing 44
Weber, Pat interview 103-108
Weber, Pat and Lynne 102, 103
Wetsuit 19
Wipe out 30, 31

Yikes! 13

About the Author

Doug Werner is the author of the internationally acclaimed Start-Up Sports series. In previous lifetimes he graduated with a Fine Arts Degree from Cal State Long Beach, built an ad agency and founded a graphics firm. In 1994 he established Tracks Publishing.

Werner lives with his wife Kathleen and daughter Joy in San Diego, California — one of the major sport funzones on the planet.

Ordering More Start-Up Sports Books:

The Start-Up Sports series:

❏ Surfer's Start-Up   ❏ Longboarder's Start-Up
❏ Snowboarder's Start-Up   ❏ Golfer's Start-Up
❏ Sailor's Start-Up   ❏ Fencer's Start-Up
❏ In-line Skater's Start-Up ❏ Boxer's Start-Up
❏ Bowler's Start-Up   ❏ Backpacker's Start-Up

Call 1-800-443-3570.
Visa and MasterCard accepted.

Start-Up Sports books are available in all major book-stores and selected sporting goods stores.

Tracks Publishing
140 Brightwood Avenue
Chula Vista, CA 91910
619-476-7125
fax 619-476-8173
tracks@startupsports.com

(**www.startupsports.com**)

Start-Up Sports®